InVisability - The Unstoppable Future

Sarah Harvey

BookLeaf
Publishing

Presentation by *BookLeaf Publishing*

Web: www.bookleafpub.com

E-mail: info@bookleafpub.com

ISBN: 9789357613552

First edition 2022

Dedication is contributed too;

*Melissa Drganc (6) at this time of
submission*

Daniel Drganc (2) at the time of submission

Sharon Bailey (NDCO) and Support

*Nichole Myers (Life long coach, support,
mentor and best friend)*

ACKNOWLEDGEMENT

I would like to:

"Before we begin, I would like to acknowledge the Traditional Owners and Custodians (the Kaurna People') of the Country on which we meet today, and their continuing connection to land, sea, and community. I pay my respects to their Elders, past present and emerging.
I would like to extend that acknowledgement and respect to any Aboriginal and Torres Strait Islander peoples here today."

PREFACE

Travel through my journey with me. It takes you through some hard and good times, it tells the truth of happiness and struggles, it defined who i am today.

First Nations

I am First Nations,
I have been fighting the systems all my life,
Stuck in the matrix of blue or red pills,
I am a mother of two,
I don't want them too fight the systems,
Systems of racism,
Violence against families,
Substance abuse,
Child safety,
Foster care,
Sexual abuse,
Workers compensation,
Trauma,
Nightmares,
Medications,
Disability,
A system where I've never felt safe.

Your so loud

Your so loud I cant think,
Ur so loud I need silence,
Ur voice over powers mine,
Why won't you listen too me,
Ur voice is so loud its drowning out the world,
Ur voice is powerful,
Ur voice is who we seek,
She will be wisdom, he will be truth,
Ur so loud I can dance,
What is all this white noise?
The world's become so loud again,
Loud on the bus,
In the shopping centre,
Why is everything so loud..

Sacrifice

She stood their and asked God..
Why does it seem so difficult for people to
understand, I am not complex but was made in
the image of a man,
Why does it feel like bricks stand in my way,
every struggle is defining who I have become
today,
Why must we continue to try and help others,
When others won't help us,
God quietly said I would never give you more
then I think you could handle,
But God she said quietly why did you pick me,
Of all the races, genders and in qualities,
I picked you because you are strengthen, love
and kindness,
You random acts will change one person at a
time, and their generosity will spread like fires,
It may not happen today, but it will happen,
You are protected by thousands of years of
ancestors,
You are protected when the universe sees,
That you are willing to sacrifice everything that
was made in my image, the mirrors of lakes,
The truth shall set you free, you will be angel..

How come it feels like my wings have been clipped,
Slowing dying and loosing my grip,
Do you know remember the nails through my hands,
When I was laughed at because I told them, I could turn water into wine,
That I could cure the sick and change time..
God she said one last time, thank you for ur sacrifice, I thank you because even with every battle I am still alive.

The year that was..

The year that was...

This was unlike any year, with fire and floods,
This was a year with a pandemic, that left our
hearts heavy,
Still recovering, still isolating, still living and
breathing,
Just as the little green shoot comes up from the
burnt ashes,
The water begins to subside.. until theirs another
warning.. I watch the clouds with my eyes, and
what's left of my home with my heart,
I pray, and I pray again..
Spare me the tears and grief,
Teach me too smile again..
You go about your day talking about I cant go to
the pub today.. whilst others embrace too loose
everything, their lives, their homes, their cars,
their businesses.. you go about your day wishing
to visit the store for new clothes.. but you walk
freely, and we have nothing in our stores.. you
are but small minded to whats happening around
you, contained in a bubble that goes as far as the
local shopping centre, the beach, or the doctor..
here I am standing with nothing left..

This was the year that sore thousands loose
relationships, the stress gained too much.. the
differences of opinion.. this is the year that
taught us not to be reliant on work, to think
about sustainable lives.. to know who was
actually their to support, and who was their to
judge.. this is the year that was..

Unstoppable..

InVisability

When something is invisible it is clear, and you
cant see it,
You cant feel it,
you cant touch it,
you cant open it,
you cant be apart of it,
I have been living with an invisible disability,
In pain for many years,
i cry when its the worst,
i cant function,
i cant work,
i cant be apart of society,
It fluctuates and sometimes its not here,
That's why its called InVisability.

The Warrior

The warrior stands in front of me,
ready to take his place,
but their are mercy waters ahead,
he leaps from one job to another,
one hunt to another,
answering all the questions asked of him,
he tells me don't worry, but i do,
sometimes he tells me fabulous news,
other days he tells me quite complex of nature
news,
but today he tells me he is a warrior,
i watch him hunt and gather,
i watch him create a sustainable life.

Seasons

Season's come and go,
and i am always left behind,
winter's on my birthday,
but i have never sen the snow,
summer is my youngest brother's,
but he doesn't talk to me,
spring is my mother and autumn my older
brother,
the season's come and go,
i see the rain, more then my family,
i see the rain more then the sun,
i see the grass grow,
but season's come and go,
just like the people in my life,
they come and go and have had their time,
i see the sun rise and set,
but it does go with guilt and regrets,
but seasons come and go,
but i am still left behind.

My time is over

I have been here before,
i know this place,
but now its time to go,
its time to realise who i am and my potential,
its time to heal the scare left unhealed,
its time to forgive the wrongs,
its time to receive love,
its time for my story
my time is over here.

A rebel

You were like a flower, that i wanted to touch,
but after realisation you are ash,
thank you for the moment where i forgot
everything,
the moment that i was complete,
your soul eased my mind,
my feet couldn't touch the ground,
I took a broken ashed flower, and gave it life,
i told you one day you would be different,
you may feel you have used me,
and taken what you think is yours,
however my friend i am an angel with a cuase.

I want a man

i want a man that makes me feel safe,
i am not perfect, but they can take me for my
true self,
someone who see my beauty whilst i have messy
hair,
and my ideas are a happy adventure,
i want a guy who will take the risk to love me,
to fall hopelessly in love,
but let me have my freedom,
and understand the journey i am taking,
i want a man that can heal all these scars with
one touch,
that will love my children as they are,
to guard me like a precious stone,
i want a man i don't need to fix, or make smile,
someone who has passions like mine,
someone who loves their family, and will build a
world with us.

Do you Remember

Do you remember being young?

Do you remember when i met you?
you promised the world to me,
do you remember your first kiss?
it felt like the world froze,
do you remember holding my hand?
remember the colours of my hair,
do you remember this little word love?
how it feel up my cup.

What will happen

What will happen in ten years time?
Who will wonder with eyes full of tears,
my daddy use to say "hold your way be strong
my little girl"
One day you will stand on your feet,
one day jump on the moon,
one day the rain will stop falling,
and the sun will come calling,
my mum she use to rock me too sleep,
id go and count my white sheep,
1,2,3,4,5....
my mum always use to say "today is just another
bad day, tomorrow the sun will rise and the pain
will go away"
everyone will see Sarah Jane,
a love that burn forever brightly, has an
unconditional love,
that love is rare it doesn't just get found.

Sorry

Do you say it like you mean it,
will it go away this pain,
do you really see it,
or is this pain going to stay,
will it happen again,
will i be high and dry my friend,
standard on an island of my own,
you say it like its a toy,
then throw it away life some decoy,
sorry means exactly that "sorry".

Im sorry

I watch you as you swam and sunk,
watched you throw your life away,
i should have tried better as a friend,
i instead wished it all away,
The hurt was not mine to bear,
our lives are short and sweet,
sometimes gone in an instance ,
i realised today we both suffered,
i hope you can forgive as i walk away.

Dreams are made of lollipops

Tonight i want to fly, up in the sky,
Tonight i want to feel free,
bathe my body in the sea,
tonight the music makes me move,
the struggles disappear, and i am in the grove,
tonight i take a box,
because i am the hottest ticket around,
tonight all i need is for you too love me,
chase me like a butterfly,
trapped i have been for such a long time,
beauty and the beast please bring me a rose,
all covered in gold,
where are all my butterfly's
what went so wrong?
dreams are made of lollipops, and rainbows,
the clouds are made of candy,
tonight i want to be free like a butterfly

Your tiny hands

like tiny drops of rain,
you dance upon my heart,
god has answered my prays and brought you too
me,
your tiny smiles keep me sober and away from
all the pain,
i love your tiny toes and hands,
i love your tiny lips and nose,
i love your giggles and the way you wake me,
you have awaked me to my journey.

The silent night

He walks the halls with a silent laughter,
collecting the tears of lost souls,
why we chase time and beauty, and just one
more day with loved ones,
we are filled with regrets, if only,
we fall with the overwhelming news,
we walk into a new year with a black cloud,
a new year already carrying devastation,
a new year carrying bundles of joy, from a door
that had to shut,
yet he sits and wait to collect all those souls,
a lost soul is not determined by death or grief
like most would assume,
lost souls are the generations with questions, and
no answers,
it is the elders with no recognition, because they
have been separated,
it is the children who sleep restlessly,
it is our unrecognised super hero's, doctors,
lawyers, police,
 we all have to take this journey,
unfortunately i have already taken mine.

Sisters United

In this balance of time you have wait to be
united,
lost due to other worlds and stranger too the
wind,
years apart and so different,
but...
a future so bright
one that holds a path to the next generation,
united we stand as sisters, that we have finally
met,
at the sadest time in our life we are united.

Turtle

you ever hear the story about the turtle and the
hair,
the hair ran through the race, but the turtle go
their,
the turtle was slow and took his time,
the hair was a rabbit that bounced all the time,
the turtle was making some decisions on the
way,
the first decision he made was what would he
wear today?
as the heir ran past "turtle your too slow"
the turtle continued to ignore and prep for the
race,
collecting his shoes, socks and other things,
the heir was running to the finish line,
the second decision of the day, was was turtle
white or black?
the heir yelled out "come on turtle your so slow,
i could win this race hands down,
the turtle didn't frown, or say no i couldn't,
he kept going one step at a time, and he was just
about at the finish line,
the turtle began to grab some speed along the
way,

heir one last time said i may have tripped but i
am still winning,
are you said the turtle..

The turtle has one last decision, let the turtle win
or let him loose and learn his lesson.

Are you sick

Are you sick mummy,
do you need a band-aide,
no mummy is pain,
mummy needs to rest,
wheres the help when i need it the most,
tats right it's not here,
its very clear.

Mummy ill have to struggle through fatigue,
mummy will have to struggle through the pain,
mummy will fall asleep, and im not trying too,
you will wake mummy,
"mummy i am hungry please feed me"
"mummy i need to change the channel"
"mammy i need you, wake up mummy"

Mummy wakes and I've forgotten where i am.

The ending

24

The ending is coming,
The ending of my studies,
the ending of my work,
the ending of struggling,
the ending of needing.

When the end does come ill be better...